© Armando Marichalar

Table of Contents:

Chapter 1: Laying the Foundation

Chapter 2: Building Your Knowledge

Chapter 3: Crafting Your Investment Plan

Chapter 4: Types of Investment Strategies

Chapter 5: Financing Your Empire

Chapter 6: Finding the Right Property

Chapter 7: Negotiating Like a Pro

Chapter 8: Managing Your Properties

Chapter 9: Scaling Your Real Estate Business

Chapter 10: Avoiding Common Pitfalls

INTRODUCTION:

Why Real Estate?

Real estate has long been a cornerstone of wealth creation. Unlike stocks or bonds, property investments offer tangible assets, opportunities for cash flow, and avenues for value appreciation. This guide is designed to provide practical strategies for beginners and seasoned investors alike, helping you unlock the potential of real estate to build a sustainable property empire.

CHAPTER 1: LAYING THE FOUNDATION

UNDERSTANDING REAL ESTATE INVESTMENT

Real estate is a broad industry offering diverse opportunities for investment. Understanding the different types of real estate is the first step toward making informed decisions. Below are the primary categories:

1. Residential Properties

Residential real estate includes single-family homes, duplexes, condos, and apartments. These properties are often the starting point for new investors because of their familiarity and relatively predictable demand. Rental income from residential properties can provide a steady cash flow while the property appreciates in value.

2. Commercial Properties

This category includes office buildings, retail spaces, and industrial properties. Commercial properties often have longer lease terms and higher returns, but they can also require more substantial capital and management expertise. Demand in this sector tends to be influenced by the broader economic climate.

3.   Mixed-Use Properties

Mixed-use properties combine residential and commercial spaces in one development, like a building with retail shops on the ground floor and apartments above. These investments can diversify income streams and mitigate risk.

4.   Vacant Land

Investing in undeveloped land can be lucrative for investors who foresee future demand in a specific area. This type of investment typically requires patience, as the land may take years to appreciate or be developed.

5.   REITs (Real Estate Investment Trusts)

For those who prefer a more hands-off approach, REITs allow investors to buy shares in companies that own, operate, or finance income-producing properties. REITs are traded on stock exchanges, providing liquidity that direct real estate investments often lack.

Why Location Matters

One of the most critical factors influencing the success of any real estate investment is location. A prime location can enhance a property's desirability, increase its rental income potential, and boost long-term appreciation. Here's what to consider when evaluating a location:

1. Proximity to Employment Opportunities

Properties near business districts, industrial parks, or other employment hubs attract tenants and buyers. A strong local economy with diverse industries is an excellent indicator of stable demand.

2. Access to Quality Schools and Healthcare

Families prioritize access to good schools and medical facilities when choosing where to live. Properties in well-regarded school districts often appreciate faster and command higher rents.

3. Transportation Infrastructure

Accessibility is crucial. Properties near public transportation, major highways, or airports are often more appealing to tenants and buyers, particularly in urban areas.

4. Local Amenities

The availability of grocery stores, restaurants, parks, and entertainment venues can significantly impact the desirability of a location. Neighborhoods with thriving local amenities tend to experience higher property values.

5. Safety and Community

A safe and well-maintained community attracts more tenants and buyers. Research crime rates and community initiatives in the area you're considering.

The Importance of Market Timing

Real estate markets are cyclical. Understanding where a market stands in its cycle can influence the success of your investment. The key stages include:

1. Recovery

During a recovery phase, the market is emerging from a downturn. Property prices are often undervalued, making this an excellent time to buy.

2. Expansion

As the economy strengthens, demand for housing and commercial space increases. Property values rise, and new developments emerge.

3. Peak

At this stage, the market experiences high demand, limited supply, and peak prices. This is often a good time to sell but a challenging time to buy.

4. Contraction

When demand slows, property prices stagnate or decline. For savvy investors, this phase can present opportunities to acquire properties at discounted rates.

Benefits of Real Estate Investment

Investing in real estate offers numerous advantages over other asset classes:

1. Tangible Asset

Unlike stocks or bonds, real estate is a physical asset that you can see, touch, and improve.

2. Cash Flow

Rental properties generate regular income that can cover expenses and contribute to profits.

3. Appreciation

Over time, properties generally increase in value, offering long-term returns.

4. Leverage Opportunities

Real estate allows you to use borrowed funds (mortgages) to control valuable assets, amplifying your potential returns.

5. Tax Benefits

Real estate investors can take advantage of tax deductions on mortgage interest, property depreciation, maintenance, and more.

6. Portfolio Diversification

Real estate often moves independently of stock markets, making it a valuable addition to an investment portfolio.

Key Considerations for Beginners

If you're new to real estate, consider the following:

1. Start Small

Begin with a single-family rental property or a small multi-unit building. Gain experience before scaling up to larger or more complex investments.

2. Learn Continuously

The real estate market evolves constantly. Stay informed by reading books, attending seminars, or seeking mentorship from experienced investors.

3. Build a Network

Relationships with real estate agents, lenders, attorneys, and contractors are invaluable. A strong network can help you find opportunities and solve problems quickly.

4. Think Long-Term

Real estate isn't a get-rich-quick scheme. Approach it with patience and a commitment to gradual growth.

By laying a solid foundation, you'll be well-equipped to navigate the complexities of real estate and begin building your property empire.

CHAPTER 2: BUILDING YOUR KNOWLEDGE

Before embarking on your real estate investment journey, equipping yourself with knowledge is critical. An informed investor is better positioned to identify opportunities, mitigate risks, and achieve long-term success. This chapter covers financial literacy, market research, and essential tools for making smart decisions.

Financial Literacy: The Cornerstone of Real Estate Success

Financial literacy is the foundation of successful real estate investing. Understanding key financial concepts helps you analyze potential investments and manage your portfolio effectively. Below are the most critical concepts to master:

1. Cash Flow

Cash flow refers to the net income generated by a property after all expenses, such as mortgage payments, property taxes, insurance, and maintenance, have been deducted. A positive cash flow property generates income that exceeds its costs, providing steady financial returns.

Example:

- Monthly Rental Income: $2,000

- Mortgage Payment: $1,200

- Property Taxes and Insurance: $300

- Maintenance: $100

- Cash Flow: $2,000 - ($1,200 + $300 + $100) = $400/month

2.   Cap Rate (Capitalization Rate)

The cap rate measures a property's annual return based on its purchase price. It's calculated as:

Cap Rate = (Net Operating Income(NOI) / Purchase Price) x 100

Investors use cap rates to compare properties in similar markets.

3.   ROI (Return on Investment)

ROI calculates the profitability of an investment over time. It's expressed as a percentage:

ROI = (Profit / Initial Investment) x 100

Understanding ROI helps you assess whether a property meets your financial goals.

4. Loan-to-Value Ratio (LTV)

LTV is the ratio of a loan amount to the appraised value of a property. Lower LTV ratios are less risky for lenders and may result in better loan terms.

LTV = (Loan Amount / Appraised Value) x 100

Market Research: Knowing the Landscape

Thorough market research is the key to identifying lucrative investment opportunities. Real estate markets vary widely, even within the same city. By understanding local dynamics, you can make smarter purchasing decisions.

1. Study Local Trends

Investigate the current trends in the areas you're considering. Questions to ask include:

- Are property values increasing or stagnating?

- What is the average time properties spend on the market?

- Is the rental market strong, or are vacancies common?

2. Understand Supply and Demand

Analyze whether demand for housing or commercial spaces exceeds supply. Areas with high demand and limited inventory typically offer better returns.

3. Evaluate Economic Indicators

The health of a local economy significantly impacts real estate markets. Look for:

- Low unemployment rates

- A diverse job market

- Infrastructure development projects

4. Study Demographics

Research the population trends in the area. Are more people moving in or leaving? Younger populations may demand rental units, while older residents may prefer downsizing or retirement communities.

Essential Research Tools

Investors have access to a wealth of tools and resources to make informed decisions. Here are some of the most effective:

1. Online Real Estate Platforms

Websites like Zillow, Realtor.com, and Redfin offer insights into property prices, rental estimates, and market trends.

2. Government Data

Access census data, crime statistics, and economic reports to understand community demographics and safety.

3. Local Real Estate Agents

Partnering with experienced agents provides insider knowledge about specific neighborhoods and off-market opportunities.

4. Networking Events

Attend real estate meetups, seminars, and conferences to connect with other investors and industry experts.

5. Market Reports

Many real estate agencies and financial institutions publish detailed market analyses. These reports often include cap rates, vacancy rates, and projected growth for specific areas.

Identifying Investment Sweet Spots

Finding the right area for investment involves more than just choosing a city or neighborhood. Look for specific signs of growth or potential:

1. Urban Revitalization Projects

Areas undergoing redevelopment or gentrification often see rapid property value increases.

2. Emerging Markets

Invest in locations with growing populations, expanding industries, and improving infrastructure. These areas offer a high potential for appreciation.

3. Undervalued Neighborhoods

Sometimes, areas adjacent to high-demand neighborhoods can be purchased at a discount and rise in value as development expands outward.

4. Proximity to Major Developments

Properties near upcoming shopping centers, schools, or transportation hubs are likely to experience increased demand and appreciation.

The Power of Comparative Market Analysis (CMA)

A Comparative Market Analysis (CMA) is a critical tool for determining the value of a property. It involves comparing a property to similar ones recently sold in the same area. The following factors are typically considered:

- Size: Square footage, number of bedrooms, and bathrooms.

- Condition: Renovations or upgrades.

- Location: Proximity to amenities and overall desirability.

- Sale Date: Properties sold within the last six months are most relevant.

CMAs help you make competitive offers without overpaying.

Avoiding Common Market Research Pitfalls

Even experienced investors can make mistakes. Here's what to watch out for:

1. Relying on Outdated Information

Real estate markets change rapidly. Ensure your data is current and reflects recent trends.

2. Ignoring Local Knowledge

National or regional trends don't always apply to specific neighborhoods. Collaborate with local experts.

3. Overlooking Future Developments

Research upcoming projects like new highways, schools, or business hubs that could significantly impact property values.

<u>Putting Knowledge Into Action</u>

The insights gained through financial literacy and market research should guide every investment decision you make. With a strong foundation of understanding, you'll be prepared to assess opportunities, negotiate effectively, and build a profitable real estate portfolio.

This knowledge is your most powerful asset—use it to make confident and calculated moves in your real estate journey.

CHAPTER 3: CRAFTING YOUR INVESTMENT PLAN

Real estate investing is not a one-size-fits-all venture. The key to long-term success lies in creating a personalized investment plan that aligns with your financial goals, risk tolerance, and available resources. This chapter will guide you through setting clear objectives, budgeting effectively, and building a roadmap for your property empire.

<u>Setting Clear Goals</u>

Before diving into the world of real estate, it's crucial to define your objectives. Ask yourself what you hope to achieve and what success looks like for you. Clear goals will help you focus your efforts and measure your progress.

1.   Income Goals

•   Are you looking for monthly cash flow from rental income, or do you prefer long-term appreciation of property value?

•   Decide how much income you aim to generate in the short term and the long term.

2. Portfolio Growth

- How many properties do you want to own within the next 5, 10, or 20 years?

- Do you plan to diversify across property types or focus on a specific niche?

3. Exit Strategy

- Determine whether you plan to hold properties indefinitely, sell them after appreciation, or pass them down as part of a legacy plan.

- Having an exit strategy helps guide your buying decisions and timelines.

4. Risk Tolerance

- Assess your comfort level with risk. For instance, high-risk investments like fix-and-flip properties may yield higher returns but require more involvement and carry greater uncertainty.

Creating a Realistic Budget

Understanding your financial situation is essential for developing a feasible investment plan. Here's how to build a comprehensive budget:

1. Calculate Your Available Capital

- Assess how much money you have for a down payment, closing costs, and initial repairs or renovations.

- Explore whether you can use equity from your primary residence or other assets as leverage.

2. Secure Financing

- Get pre-approved for a mortgage to understand your borrowing capacity.

- Research different loan options, such as conventional loans, FHA loans, or private lending, to find the best fit.

3. Account for Additional Costs

- Closing Costs: Typically 2-5% of the property price, covering legal fees, appraisal, and title insurance.

- Renovations: Factor in the cost of repairs or upgrades if you're purchasing a fixer-upper.

- Maintenance: Budget 1-2% of the property's value annually for ongoing maintenance.

- Property Taxes and Insurance: Research local rates to estimate these recurring expenses.

4. Emergency Fund

- Set aside a contingency fund for unexpected expenses such as major repairs or vacancies.

Choosing Your Investment Strategy

Your investment plan should reflect the type of real estate strategy you want to pursue. Different strategies align with varying goals, time commitments, and risk levels.

1. Buy-and-Hold Strategy

- Ideal for investors seeking steady rental income and long-term appreciation.

- Focus on properties in areas with stable rental demand and potential for growth.

2. Fix-and-Flip

- Buy undervalued properties, renovate them, and sell for a profit.

- This strategy requires market knowledge, renovation expertise, and the ability to act quickly.

3. House Hacking

- Purchase a multi-unit property, live in one unit, and rent out the others to offset your living costs.

- A low-risk strategy that allows you to build equity while covering expenses.

4. Vacation Rentals

- Invest in short-term rental properties in popular tourist destinations.

- This strategy can generate higher income than traditional rentals but may require active management.

5. BRRRR Method (Buy, Rehab, Rent, Refinance, Repeat)

- Acquire distressed properties, renovate them, rent them out, and refinance to recover your initial investment.

- Use the funds to reinvest in additional properties, scaling your portfolio.

Setting a Timeline for Success

A realistic timeline helps you stay on track and achieve your goals in stages. Here's an example:

1. First Year

- Learn the basics of real estate investing through courses, books, and mentorship.

- Save for a down payment and improve your credit score.

- Purchase your first property and focus on managing it effectively.

2. Years 2-5

- Expand your portfolio by reinvesting profits and leveraging equity.

- Diversify your investments by exploring different property types or locations.

- Build a team of professionals, including agents, contractors, and accountants.

3. Years 5-10

- Focus on scaling your operations, optimizing cash flow, and reducing debt.

- Consider moving into larger or commercial properties to increase returns.

- Develop passive income streams through property management companies or REITs.

The Role of Market Research in Your Plan

Your investment plan should be flexible enough to adapt to changing market conditions. Regularly update your research on:

- Local property values

- Rental demand and vacancy rates

- Economic factors influencing your target markets

Adjust your strategy if market conditions change, such as pivoting from flipping to buy-and-hold during a market downturn.

Aligning Your Plan with Your Personal Life

Real estate investing requires time, effort, and resources. Consider how it fits into your overall lifestyle:

- Time Commitment: How much time can you dedicate to managing properties, finding deals, or overseeing renovations?

- Family Goals: Discuss your investment plan with your family to ensure it aligns with shared priorities.

- Flexibility: Build a plan that accommodates unexpected life changes, such as job relocations or financial emergencies.

Tracking Progress and Staying Accountable

Regularly review your progress to ensure you're on track. Use tools like:

- Spreadsheets to monitor income, expenses, and cash flow.

- Financial Software like QuickBooks or specialized real estate apps to analyze performance.

- Vision Boards or written goals to stay motivated and focused.

Conclusion

Crafting a solid investment plan is like designing a blueprint for your property empire. It provides clarity, structure, and direction while allowing you to adapt to market dynamics. By setting clear goals, creating a realistic budget, and choosing the right strategy, you'll be prepared to take actionable steps toward building a successful real estate portfolio. With a well-crafted plan, your journey toward financial freedom begins with confidence and purpose.

CHAPTER 4: TYPES OF INVESTMENT STRATEGIES

When it comes to real estate investing, there are many paths to building wealth. Choosing the right investment strategy depends on your financial goals, risk tolerance, available capital, and the time you're willing to dedicate. This chapter explores the most popular real estate investment strategies, breaking down how they work, their pros and cons, and tips for success.

1. <u>Buy-and-Hold Strategy</u>

The buy-and-hold strategy involves purchasing properties and holding them for an extended period while earning rental income and benefiting from property appreciation.

How It Works:

•   Purchase a property in a desirable or emerging market.

•   Rent it out to tenants to generate steady cash flow.

•   Over time, the property value increases, allowing you to build equity.

Pros:

•   Reliable income stream through rent.

- Long-term appreciation builds wealth.

- Tax benefits, including depreciation and mortgage interest deductions.

Cons:

- Requires property management or outsourcing to a management company.

- Risk of vacancies or tenant issues.

- Initial costs, such as down payments and maintenance, can be significant.

Tips for Success:

- Invest in areas with strong rental demand and potential for growth.

- Screen tenants thoroughly to avoid payment and maintenance issues.

- Regularly maintain the property to retain its value.

2. Fix-and-Flip Strategy

The fix-and-flip strategy focuses on purchasing undervalued or distressed properties, renovating them, and selling them for a profit within a short timeframe.

How It Works:

- Identify a property below market value that needs cosmetic or structural improvements.

- Renovate the property to enhance its appeal and market value.

- Sell the upgraded property at a higher price.

Pros:

- Quick returns, often within months.

- Opportunities to build capital for future investments.

- Allows creative freedom in property design and improvement.

Cons:

- High risk due to market fluctuations or unexpected renovation costs.

- Requires expertise in construction and market trends.

- Capital gains taxes on profits.

Tips for Success:

- Work with experienced contractors and adhere to a strict budget.

- Analyze comparable properties (comps) to estimate the post-renovation value accurately.

- Ensure a strong buyer demand in the local market.

3. House Hacking

House hacking involves living in one part of a property while renting out other units to offset living costs or generate income.

How It Works:

- Purchase a multi-family property or a single-family home with additional rental spaces (e.g., a basement apartment).

- Live in one unit and rent out the others.

- Use the rental income to cover the mortgage and other expenses.

Pros:

- Reduces or eliminates housing costs.
- Builds equity while generating income.
- Ideal for first-time investors with limited capital.

Cons:

- Requires living alongside tenants, which can impact privacy.
- May involve tenant management responsibilities.
- Limited scalability unless you move out and repeat the process.

Tips for Success:

- Choose properties with high rental demand and affordable mortgage payments.
- Be prepared to manage tenant relationships and property maintenance.
- Use FHA loans, which often require lower down payments, to get started.

4. Short-Term Rentals (Vacation Rentals)

This strategy involves purchasing properties to rent out on a short-term basis, often through platforms like Airbnb or Vrbo.

How It Works:

- Invest in a property located in a high-demand tourist area or city.

- Furnish the property and list it on short-term rental platforms.

- Manage bookings and provide a high-quality guest experience.

Pros:

- Higher income potential compared to long-term rentals.

- Flexibility to use the property for personal vacations.

- Diversification of your investment portfolio.

Cons:

- Highly dependent on location and seasonal demand.

- Requires active management or outsourcing to a short-term rental manager.

- Subject to local regulations and restrictions on short-term rentals.

Tips for Success:

- Focus on areas with year-round demand, such as urban centers or destinations with diverse attractions.

- Offer unique amenities or experiences to attract guests.

- Stay updated on local laws governing short-term rentals.

5. BRRRR Strategy (Buy, Rehab, Rent, Refinance, Repeat)

The BRRRR method is a popular strategy for building a scalable portfolio with minimal upfront capital.

How It Works:

- Buy: Acquire a distressed or undervalued property.

- Rehab: Renovate the property to increase its value and rental appeal.

- Rent: Find tenants and generate steady rental income.

- Refinance: Use a cash-out refinance to recover your initial investment.

- Repeat: Reinvest the recovered capital into additional properties.

Pros:

- Efficient use of capital, allowing for portfolio growth.

- Builds equity and generates cash flow simultaneously.

- Reduces risk by refinancing after stabilizing the property.

Cons:

- Requires significant knowledge of financing and renovation.

- Relies on accurate post-renovation appraisals.

- Can be time-intensive, especially during the rehab phase.

Tips for Success:

- Work with reliable contractors and lenders who understand the BRRRR process.

- Focus on properties in areas with strong rental markets.

- Be realistic about timelines and costs during renovations

6. Commercial Real Estate

Commercial real estate investing involves properties used for business purposes, such as offices, retail spaces, or industrial facilities.

How It Works:

- Purchase or develop a property that can generate income through leasing to businesses.

- Negotiate long-term leases for consistent cash flow.

- Benefit from property appreciation and stable tenant relationships.

Pros:

- Longer lease terms provide stable income.

- Potentially higher returns compared to residential properties.

- Tenants often handle maintenance and utilities through net leases.

Cons:

- Requires significant upfront capital and expertise.

- Market demand fluctuates with economic conditions.

- Longer vacancies can occur if tenants leave.

Tips for Success:

- Research the local business environment and tenant demand.

- Diversify across property types (e.g., office, retail, industrial) to reduce risk.

- Consider partnering with experienced commercial real estate investors.

7. Real Estate Wholesaling

Wholesaling involves identifying properties below market value and assigning the purchase contract to another buyer for a fee.

How It Works:

- Find motivated sellers willing to sell at a discount.

- Negotiate a contract to purchase the property.

- Assign the contract to an end buyer, such as a flipper or investor.

Pros:

- Low capital requirement since you don't need to buy the property.

- Quick turnaround for profits.

- Minimal risk compared to holding or flipping properties.

Cons:

- Requires strong negotiation and marketing skills.

- Limited profit margins compared to other strategies.

- Success depends on a network of motivated sellers and buyers.

Tips for Success:

- Build a database of potential buyers before finding deals.

- Use marketing tools to reach distressed property owners.

- Master local real estate laws governing assignment contracts.

Choosing the Right Strategy for You

Selecting the right strategy depends on several factors:

1. Your Financial Goals: Are you looking for quick profits, steady cash flow, or long-term wealth building?

2. Time Commitment: Do you prefer hands-on management or passive income streams?

3. Risk Tolerance: Are you comfortable with higher-risk strategies like flipping, or do you prefer stable investments like buy-and-hold?

4. Available Capital: Some strategies, like BRRRR or commercial investing, require more upfront capital.

By understanding these strategies and their unique advantages, you can craft an investment plan that aligns with your personal goals and resources. Remember, real estate investing is a journey, and your strategy may evolve as you gain experience and build confidence.

CHAPTER 5: FINANCING YOUR EMPIRE

Financing is the backbone of real estate investing. Building a property empire requires access to capital, a solid understanding of funding options, and the ability to leverage other people's money effectively. This chapter delves into traditional and creative financing methods, the importance of creditworthiness, and strategies for optimizing your funding opportunities.

<ins>Understanding the Basics of Real Estate Financing</ins>

Real estate financing involves using borrowed money to purchase properties, leveraging debt to maximize your investment potential. The goal is to secure funding with terms that align with your investment strategy while maintaining manageable risks.

1.	Key Concepts in Real Estate Financing

•	Loan-to-Value Ratio (LTV): The percentage of the property's value financed by a loan. For example, an 80% LTV means you provide a 20% down payment.

•	Debt Service Coverage Ratio (DSCR): A measure of a property's cash flow relative to its debt obligations. A DSCR above 1 indicates sufficient income to cover debts.

- Amortization: The process of paying off debt through regular payments over time.

2. Why Financing is Crucial

- Amplifies buying power, allowing you to acquire more properties.

- Spreads risk by minimizing upfront capital requirements.

- Enables scalability and long-term portfolio growth.

Traditional Financing Options

Traditional financing methods are commonly used by real estate investors due to their predictability and relatively low costs.

1. Conventional Loans

- Offered by banks and mortgage lenders, these loans typically require a 20–25% down payment for investment properties.

- Competitive interest rates and fixed payment schedules make them appealing.

2. FHA Loans (Federal Housing Administration)

- FHA loans are government-backed and require as little as a 3.5% down payment.

- Ideal for first-time investors or those with lower credit scores.

- These loans are primarily for owner-occupied properties but can be used for multi-family homes if you live in one unit.

3. VA Loans (Veterans Affairs)

- Available to eligible military personnel and veterans, VA loans offer no down payment and favorable terms.

- Like FHA loans, these must be used for owner-occupied properties.

4. Portfolio Loans

- These are loans kept by banks rather than sold on the secondary market, offering flexible terms.

- Useful for investors with unique financial situations or those purchasing multiple properties.

5. Commercial Loans

- Designed for larger residential properties (5+ units) or commercial real estate.

- Higher interest rates and shorter terms but tailored to the property's income potential rather than the borrower's credit.

Creative Financing Strategies

For investors looking to minimize upfront capital or overcome traditional financing barriers, creative financing can open doors to new opportunities.

1. Seller Financing

- The property seller acts as the lender, offering you a loan to purchase the property.

- Negotiable terms, lower closing costs, and no need for traditional lenders.

2. Hard Money Loans

- Short-term, high-interest loans provided by private lenders.

- Commonly used for fix-and-flip projects where speed and flexibility are crucial.

3. Private Money Lending

- Loans from individuals (friends, family, or investors) rather than institutions.

- Terms and interest rates are often negotiable based on trust and relationship.

4. Lease Option (Rent-to-Own)

- Rent a property with the option to buy it at a predetermined price later.

- A portion of the rent may be applied to the purchase price, allowing you to secure the property while building capital.

5. Partnerships and Joint Ventures

- Collaborate with other investors to pool resources and share risks.

- Clearly define roles, responsibilities, and profit-sharing agreements upfront.

6. Equity Financing

- Instead of borrowing money, sell a portion of the property's equity to investors.

- Useful for high-value or commercial properties.

The Role of Credit in Real Estate Financing

Your credit score and history play a significant role in securing favorable financing terms. Here's how to optimize your creditworthiness:

1. Improve Your Credit Score

- Pay bills on time and reduce outstanding debt.

- Avoid applying for multiple loans or credit cards within a short period.

- Monitor your credit report for errors and dispute inaccuracies.

2. Build Financial Reserves

- Lenders favor borrowers with ample savings to cover emergencies or unexpected expenses.

- Maintain at least 3–6 months of mortgage payments as a reserve.

3. Demonstrate Stability

- Show consistent income and employment history.

- Keep detailed records of your real estate experience, especially if you're a seasoned investor.

Leverage: Maximizing Your Returns

Leverage involves using borrowed funds to increase your investment potential. While it can amplify returns, it also increases risk.

1. Benefits of Leverage

- Increased Purchasing Power: Enables you to acquire properties you couldn't afford outright.

- Higher ROI: Magnifies returns when property values and rental income rise.

- Diversification: Spreads your capital across multiple properties.

2. Risks of Leverage

- Debt Obligations: Loan repayments must be made regardless of cash flow or market conditions.

- Market Volatility: A downturn in property values could reduce equity or lead to losses.

3. Strategies to Manage Leverage

- Use conservative LTV ratios to maintain a safety buffer.

- Invest in cash-flow-positive properties to cover debt payments.

- Refinance or sell underperforming properties to reduce debt.

Advanced Financing Techniques

Seasoned investors often use advanced techniques to optimize their funding and grow their portfolios.

1. Cross-Collateralization

- Use equity from one property as collateral for financing another.

- Reduces the need for large cash down payments.

2. Lines of Credit

- Establish a home equity line of credit (HELOC) or a business line of credit to access funds when needed.

- Flexible borrowing terms make these options ideal for ongoing projects.

3. Cash-Out Refinancing

- Refinance an existing property to extract its equity and reinvest in new properties.

- Works well for BRRRR (Buy, Rehab, Rent, Refinance, Repeat) strategies.

4. Syndication

- Pool funds from multiple investors to acquire large-scale properties.

- Often used for commercial or multi-family developments.

Optimizing Financing for Long-Term Success

To build a sustainable property empire, focus on strategies that align with your growth objectives:

1. Diversify Funding Sources: Use a mix of traditional and creative financing to maximize flexibility.

2. Monitor Interest Rates: Lock in favorable rates when possible to minimize costs.

3. Build Strong Relationships: Develop connections with lenders, private investors, and financial institutions to access better deals.

Conclusion

Financing your property empire is as much about strategy as it is about securing capital. By understanding the various funding options, improving your creditworthiness, and leveraging creative techniques, you can create a financial foundation that supports both immediate and long-term goals. Remember, the key is to strike a balance between maximizing opportunities and managing risks effectively. With the right approach, your financing strategy will propel you toward real estate success.

CHAPTER 6: FINDING THE RIGHT PROPERTY

Finding the right property is a critical step in building a successful real estate empire. The perfect investment is more than just a structure; it's a combination of location, property type, market trends, condition, and potential profitability. In this chapter, we'll explore how to identify profitable properties, analyze market conditions, evaluate key property characteristics, and utilize strategies to locate hidden opportunities.

<u>Understanding the Fundamentals of Property Selection</u>

Selecting the right property is about aligning your investment strategy with the market, finances, and your goals. A common mistake many investors make is rushing into purchases without properly evaluating whether a property fits their investment strategy.

1. Define Your Investment Goals

Before searching for a property, be clear about your objectives. Different strategies align with different property types. Ask yourself:

- Do I want steady cash flow or capital appreciation?

Steady cash flow properties focus on rental income, while capital appreciation properties focus on future resale value.

- Am I focusing on short-term profits or long-term wealth building?

Short-term strategies like flipping prioritize finding undervalued properties and renovating quickly, while long-term strategies like buy-and-hold focus on properties with appreciation potential and consistent income streams.

Your goals will help you determine which property type, market, and financing strategy are most appropriate.

Key Factors to Consider When Finding the Right Property

To ensure you find a successful investment property, you must evaluate several critical factors. These elements will dictate whether a property will deliver the returns you want.

1. Location, Location, Location

The location of a property is one of the most significant factors influencing its success. A great property in the wrong location will struggle to appreciate or generate consistent income.

Key Factors That Define Good Locations

•	Economic Stability: Look for areas with job growth, infrastructure projects, and economic expansion.

•	Rental Demand: Proximity to schools, hospitals, and urban centers can make a location more attractive for renters.

•	Quality of Life: Good schools, low crime rates, and access to amenities like parks and shopping centers attract families and tenants.

•	Transportation Links: Properties near airports, major highways, or public transit options are highly desirable.

Research Tools for Location Analysis:

•	Local market reports.

•	Demographic trends.

•	Real estate platforms like Zillow, Realtor.com, or Redfin.

•	City planning documents to track upcoming developments.

2. Property Type

Different property types cater to different investment strategies. Choosing the right property type depends on your goals and market analysis.

Common Property Types for Real Estate Investing:

1. Single-Family Homes:

- Ideal for long-term buy-and-hold strategies or house hacking.

- Steady demand, especially in suburban areas, due to affordability and family living needs.

2. Multi-Family Properties (Duplexes, Triplexes, & Apartments):

- These properties provide multiple income streams and economies of scale.

- A great option for buy-and-hold strategies or BRRRR investing.

3. Commercial Properties:

•   Includes office spaces, retail centers, warehouses, and industrial properties.

•   These offer longer lease agreements and potentially higher returns.

4. Vacation/Short-Term Rentals:

•   Popular in tourist areas and urban hubs.

•   Leverage platforms like Airbnb or Vrbo for marketing.

5. Land or Raw Development Property:

•   Opportunities to develop new properties or sell land to other developers.

•   Requires substantial capital but can yield high returns if done correctly.

Choosing the right property type depends on your market research, financial situation, and long-term goals. For instance, commercial spaces may provide greater cash flow opportunities but can be riskier during economic downturns.

3. Market Trends and Timing

Real estate markets fluctuate depending on the economy, demographics, and consumer demand. Understanding market trends will help you time your purchase for maximum profitability.

Analyze the Following Market Trends:

- Economic indicators like job growth and wage trends.

- Population growth in the area.

- Seasonal trends (certain areas may have cyclical demand for rentals).

- Supply and demand levels in a specific market.

Ask Yourself:

- Is the market appreciating or depreciating?

- Are there new infrastructure projects or employment hubs planned for the area?

- What is the vacancy rate? (Low vacancy rates suggest high demand for housing.)

Pro Tip: Always stay ahead of market cycles by conducting comparative market analyses (CMAs) and reviewing historical trends to identify opportunities.

4. Property Condition & Value

When searching for the right property, it's essential to evaluate its condition and how much work, if any, will be necessary to bring it up to market standards. Look at:

a. Properties That Require Rehab:

These properties can be excellent opportunities for fix-and-flip strategies or BRRRR methods. They can be purchased at a discount, improved, and resold or rented for higher returns.

What to Look For:

- Structural damage.

- Outdated features that affect marketability.

- Cosmetic damage that can be improved through renovation.

b. Move-In Ready Properties:

These properties are in good condition and are ready for renters or buyers without major renovations. They align well with buy-and-hold strategies or short-term rentals.

Property Valuation Methods:

When assessing a property's value, use these strategies:

1. Comparative Market Analysis (CMA): Compare the property with recent sales of similar homes in the area.

2. Income Approach: Analyze the property's potential rental income to determine its fair value.

3. Replacement Cost Approach: Estimate how much it would cost to replace the property with an identical one.

5. Rental Income Potential

When searching for the right property, consider its ability to generate consistent cash flow through rental income. Calculate the following:

Key Metrics to Analyze:

1. Rent vs. Mortgage Payments:

- Ensure monthly rent is enough to cover mortgage, taxes, insurance, and maintenance costs.

2. Cash Flow Analysis:

- Cash flow = Rental income - Operating expenses - Mortgage payments

3. Occupancy Rates:

- Evaluate how often properties in that area remain occupied.

Pro Tip: Target areas with a history of stable employment opportunities, as renters are more likely to stay long-term.

6. Leverage Your Network to Find Hidden Opportunities

Finding great properties isn't just about searching online or exploring listings. Tap into your personal network, professional network, and local connections:

Networking Opportunities:

- Local real estate agents.

- Wholesalers who find discounted properties.

- Local real estate investment groups.

- Property auctions.

- Off-market sellers looking for quick transactions.

Build relationships with key players, as word-of-mouth and referrals often lead to the best investment opportunities.

Conducting Due Diligence

Once you've identified a potential property, conduct comprehensive research to verify its profitability and feasibility:

1. Market Analysis: Confirm trends, rental demand, and property appreciation potential.

2. Property Inspections: Hire professionals to inspect for structural issues or costly repairs.

3. Legal Review: Ensure there are no liens, zoning issues, or pending disputes.

4. Financial Analysis: Use cash flow projections, property taxes, and mortgage costs to ensure profitability.

Completing this step can prevent costly mistakes and ensure you only move forward with investments that align with your strategy.

Conclusion

Finding the right property combines strategy, research, market trends, and due diligence. Every investor has unique objectives, but successful real estate investing hinges on identifying opportunities that align with your financial goals, strategy, and market understanding.

Whether it's a fix-and-flip, buy-and-hold, short-term rental, or commercial investment, the key to finding the right property lies in preparation, patience, and persistence. When you pair the right strategy with thorough research, market knowledge, and strategic evaluation, your search will yield profitable opportunities that can help you build your property empire.

CHAPTER 7: NEGOTIATING LIKE A PRO

Negotiation is both an art and a science. In real estate, mastering negotiation skills can mean the difference between landing a lucrative deal or walking away from an opportunity. Whether you're purchasing a property, securing financing, or negotiating rental agreements, negotiation is a skill you'll need to fine-tune to become a successful real estate investor.

This chapter will explore the principles of negotiation, key strategies, psychological tactics, and the mindset you must adopt to negotiate effectively and create win-win situations that will advance your property empire.

<u>Understanding the Role of Negotiation in Real Estate</u>

Negotiation is a vital skill for real estate investors because every property transaction involves multiple parties with different objectives, priorities, and goals. Successful negotiation allows you to:

1. Secure Better Purchase Prices: Reducing the purchase price means more equity and potential profit.

2. Structure Favorable Terms: Ensure loan terms, closing dates, contingencies, and seller concessions align with your strategy.

3.   Build Relationships: Establish trust and credibility with sellers, agents, and financial partners.

4.   Create Win-Win Situations: You can negotiate terms that satisfy all parties while maintaining relationships for future opportunities.

Understanding that negotiation is not just about "winning" but finding mutually beneficial solutions will set the foundation for long-term success in real estate investing.

The Core Principles of Successful Negotiation

Before diving into specific strategies, let's explore some core principles that successful negotiators apply consistently:

1. Do Your Homework

Preparation is the backbone of negotiation. The more information you have, the stronger your position will be.

What to Research Before Negotiating:

•   Property Value: Study comparative market analysis (CMA) to understand the fair market value.

•   Seller's Motivation: Determine why the seller is selling (moving for a job, downsizing, financial strain, inherited property, etc.). Understanding their motivations can give you leverage.

- Market Conditions: Is the market a buyer's market or a seller's market? This will influence how much room you have to negotiate.

- Loan and Financing Options: Know your financing options and be prepared to discuss financing contingencies.

- Local Market Trends: Study whether property values are increasing or declining and whether the neighborhood has potential appreciation or high rental demand.

Pro Tip: Knowledge not only gives you confidence but also allows you to make informed decisions during negotiation.

2. Establish Clear Objectives

Define your ideal outcome and identify your "walk-away point" before entering negotiations. Your objectives could include:

- Getting the lowest purchase price possible.

- Securing a favorable closing date.

- Obtaining seller concessions (covering closing costs, repairs, etc.).

- Getting favorable financing terms or lease agreements.

Knowing what you're aiming for—and what you'll settle for—creates boundaries that prevent you from becoming emotionally compromised during negotiations.

3. Build Trust and Establish Rapport

People are more likely to negotiate favorably when they trust and feel a connection with the other party. Building rapport can take the negotiation from adversarial to collaborative.

Ways to Build Trust:

- Show genuine interest in their needs or motivations.

- Communicate respectfully and empathetically.

- Listen actively to understand their perspective.

- Be transparent when appropriate.

Negotiation is much easier when the other party sees you as fair and reasonable rather than combative.

4. Aim for Win-Win Outcomes

The best negotiations create value for both parties. This doesn't mean compromising on your goals but finding creative solutions that satisfy both sides' priorities.

How to Create Win-Win Situations:

- Understand the seller's needs and priorities.

- Offer solutions that address their concerns, such as allowing a flexible closing date or covering repair costs.

- Be flexible with contingencies and terms while maintaining your objectives.

By focusing on shared goals, you foster goodwill and build long-lasting partnerships.

Essential Negotiation Strategies

Once you understand the foundational principles, implement these proven negotiation strategies to strengthen your position:

1. Start With an Anchored Offer

An "anchor" is the initial number or term you propose, and it serves as a reference point during negotiation.

How Anchoring Works:

- Present an initial offer that is strategic but reasonable. This sets the tone for the negotiation.

- For instance, if a property is listed at $300,000, you might make an initial offer of $270,000. Even if you don't settle at $270,000, the negotiation will likely revolve around that range.

Pro Tip: Make sure your initial offer is based on data from market analysis and your investment goals.

2. Use Silence Strategically

One of the most powerful negotiation tactics is the strategic use of silence. When you propose an offer, pause and give the other party time to respond. Silence can create pressure, making the other party more likely to make a counteroffer or accept your terms.

3. Leverage Contingencies

Contingencies can protect your interests while providing the flexibility needed to make negotiations successful. These include:

- Inspection Contingency: Allows you to back out of a deal or negotiate repair costs if problems are found during inspection.

- Financing Contingency: Gives you the option to exit the contract if financing fails to materialize.

- Appraisal Contingency: Protects you if the appraisal comes in below the purchase price.

These can strengthen your position by showing sellers you are thoughtful, informed, and not desperate.

4. Be Ready to Walk Away

One of the strongest positions in negotiation is the ability to walk away if the terms don't meet your goals. Avoid appearing desperate, as this can weaken your negotiating power.

How Walking Away Can Help You:

- It signals confidence and establishes that you're not desperate.

- It gives the other party a reason to make their terms more attractive to you.

- It preserves your financial and strategic flexibility by preventing you from overextending yourself.

Always be prepared to step back and revisit your strategy if needed.

5. Know When to Compromise

While walking away is a strategic tool, knowing when to compromise is equally essential. Sometimes it's worth making minor concessions to close the deal and move forward with your investment.

Examples of Concessions:

- Agreeing to a slightly higher price in exchange for a shorter closing period.

- Accepting a property "as-is" with fewer repairs in exchange for a reduced purchase price.

The key is finding compromises that align with your ultimate objectives without jeopardizing your strategy.

Psychological Tactics in Negotiation

Negotiation is not only about numbers; it's about human psychology. Understanding the mindset of the seller can give you the upper hand.

1. Use Reciprocity

People feel inclined to return favors. For example, if you're willing to offer a small benefit to the seller (e.g., a quick closing date), they may be more willing to make concessions.

2. Appeal to Emotions (When Appropriate)

Appealing to the seller's emotions can sometimes work. For example, emphasizing how much you value the home and its history may encourage them to accept your terms.

3. Establish Social Proof

Demonstrate credibility by referencing similar transactions or showing your experience. For instance, "I've worked with over 20 sellers in this neighborhood with smooth transactions."

Conclusion

Negotiation is both a science and a skill, and with consistent practice, you can sharpen this skill to secure better deals and long-term success. Always approach negotiations with preparation, clear goals, and strategic flexibility. Understand your priorities, communicate effectively, and maintain a collaborative mindset.

By mastering negotiation, you'll build a reputation as a fair, professional, and strategic investor—qualities that can lead to more deals, more partnerships, and a thriving property empire.

CHAPTER 8: MANAGING YOUR PROPERTIES

Once you've successfully acquired your properties, the next step is to focus on property management. Managing your properties effectively is critical to ensuring consistent income, maintaining your assets' value, and fostering positive relationships with tenants. Whether you own one property or dozens, efficient property management will save you time, resources, and headaches in the long run.

This chapter will outline the essential aspects of managing your real estate investments, including tenant screening, maintenance, handling finances, implementing property management systems, and dealing with common challenges.

The Role of Property Management

Property management involves overseeing the daily operations of your rental properties to ensure they run smoothly and remain profitable. Successful property management focuses on:

1.   Maintaining Occupancy: Keeping tenants in place reduces the costs associated with turnover and lost income.

2.   Ensuring Timely Rent Payments: Regularly collecting rent ensures cash flow for mortgage payments, maintenance, and other expenses.

3.   Handling Repairs & Maintenance: Properties must be well-maintained to retain their value and tenant satisfaction.

4.   Resolving Conflicts: Responding to tenant concerns promptly builds trust and reduces issues escalating into legal disputes.

5.   Managing Financials: Budgeting for expenses, taxes, and profit tracking ensures that your properties remain profitable.

Real estate investors can choose to manage their properties themselves or hire a professional property management company. This decision will depend on time, expertise, and the number of properties in your portfolio.

Tenant Screening: The Foundation of Successful Property Management

One of the most important aspects of managing properties is ensuring you select the right tenants. Proper tenant screening minimizes risks, reduces turnover, and establishes a stable income stream.

Key Elements of Tenant Screening:

1. Background Check:

Conduct a criminal background check to ensure you're renting to individuals with a responsible history.

2. Credit Report:

Review credit scores and financial history to determine if the tenant has a history of timely rent payments or has defaulted on financial obligations.

3. Employment & Income Verification:

Confirm a tenant's income to ensure they can afford the rent. A common rule is that rent should not exceed 30% of the tenant's monthly income.

4. Rental History:

Ask for references from previous landlords to gain insight into the tenant's behavior and responsibility.

5. Personal Interview:

Meet potential tenants in person (or virtually) to assess their behavior, expectations, and willingness to maintain the property.

Pro Tips for Tenant Screening:

1. Have a Clear & Consistent Screening Process:

- Avoid discriminatory practices by applying uniform screening policies to all applicants.

- Refer to federal and state laws like the Fair Housing Act.

2. Ask for a Security Deposit:

- A security deposit provides financial protection in case of damages or unpaid rent. Ensure you comply with local laws regarding the amount.

3. Require a Written Lease:

- Clearly outline the responsibilities of both parties in a detailed, legally binding lease.

Rent Collection: Timely & Efficient

Collecting rent on time is vital for ensuring cash flow, which allows you to pay mortgages, taxes, insurance, and other operational costs.

Methods for Efficient Rent Collection:

    1.   Online Rent Payment Systems:

Modern tenants expect convenience. Online platforms such as Rentec Direct, AppFolio, or Buildium allow tenants to pay rent electronically and securely.

    2.   Set Clear Due Dates:

Establish a clear payment schedule and ensure that all tenants know when rent is due and the consequences of late payments.

    3.   Offer Multiple Payment Options:

While online payments are efficient, some tenants may prefer checks, money orders, or other forms of payment.

Maintenance: Keeping Properties in Good Condition

Maintenance keeps your properties safe, habitable, and attractive to tenants. Regular maintenance reduces costly, emergency repairs while ensuring tenant satisfaction.

A Proactive Maintenance Strategy:

1. Regular Inspections:

- Perform annual or semi-annual inspections to identify problems early.

- Inspect the HVAC system, plumbing, appliances, and roofing for wear and tear.

2. Address Maintenance Requests Promptly:

- Respond quickly to tenant repair requests to prevent small issues from becoming major ones.

- Create a maintenance schedule for regular upkeep (e.g., changing air filters, inspecting smoke detectors).

3. Keep an Emergency Fund for Repairs:

- Allocate funds to deal with unexpected repairs, such as broken HVAC systems or roof leaks.

Build Relationships with Vendors:

Having a network of reliable contractors, plumbers, electricians, and repair specialists can ensure quick response times and fair pricing when maintenance issues arise.

Financial Management: Budgeting for Success

Managing finances effectively is essential to the long-term success of your real estate business. Proper financial management ensures you maximize cash flow, minimize expenses, and are prepared for unexpected costs.

Key Financial Tasks for Property Managers:

1. Track Income & Expenses:

• Categorize and track all income and expenses using accounting software like QuickBooks or property management systems.

2. Set a Maintenance Budget:

• Allocate a percentage of your rental income (e.g., 5-10%) for maintenance and unexpected repairs.

3. Plan for Capital Expenditures:

- Capital expenditures include costs like roof replacements or HVAC system upgrades. These expenses should be planned for over time.

4. Prepare for Taxes:

- Keep track of deductible expenses, such as mortgage interest, insurance, depreciation, and repair costs. Consult a tax advisor for guidance.

Handle Tenant Disputes & Evictions

Even with excellent tenant screening and maintenance policies, conflicts can arise. Property managers must be equipped to address disputes professionally and ethically.

Common Tenant Issues:

1. Late Rent Payments: Send reminders or implement a late fee policy if necessary.

2. Property Damage: Address damages promptly and evaluate whether the security deposit will cover the costs.

3. Noise Complaints: Mediate conflicts while maintaining tenant privacy.

4. Lease Violations: Address breaches (e.g., unauthorized pets or subletting) by reminding tenants of their lease obligations.

When Evictions Are Necessary:

Eviction should always be a last resort. If legal action becomes necessary:

1. Familiarize yourself with state and local eviction laws.

2. Serve proper notices (e.g., Pay or Quit Notice, Notice to Cure, or Unconditional Quit Notice).

3. Consult with a real estate attorney to ensure compliance with legal processes.

Implementing Property Management Systems

Efficient property management relies on organization and streamlined processes. Property management software can be invaluable tools for investors with multiple properties.

Top Property Management Software Options:

1. Buildium: Comprehensive for accounting, maintenance, and tenant tracking.

2. AppFolio: Combines accounting, communication, and online payment capabilities.

3. TenantCloud: Simple for small landlords with tracking tools and payment reminders.

Benefits of Property Management Systems:

- Automates rent collection.

- Tracks maintenance requests.

- Centralizes tenant data and lease agreements.

- Generates financial reports for easier tax planning.

Conclusion

Managing your properties effectively requires a mix of preparation, communication, financial oversight, and strategic planning. Whether you're managing one single-family rental or dozens of multifamily units, implementing systems and strategies will save you time and ensure your properties remain profitable.

By focusing on tenant satisfaction, maintenance, financial clarity, and prompt conflict resolution, you create the foundation for a thriving real estate portfolio. With excellent property management, your tenants stay happy, your properties retain their value, and your real estate empire will grow and flourish.

CHAPTER 9: SCALING YOUR REAL ESTATE BUSINESS

Scaling your real estate business is about taking your investments, strategies, and systems from a small, manageable operation to a thriving, profitable enterprise that generates sustainable wealth. While growing a real estate portfolio offers exciting opportunities, it also involves strategic planning, leveraging resources, and optimizing business operations to achieve efficiency and profitability.

This chapter will outline proven strategies, key methods, and actionable steps to scale your real estate business successfully. Whether you're starting with a few properties or have already established a foundation, this chapter will provide insights into systems, partnerships, strategies, and financial planning that will enable you to expand your real estate empire.

Why Scale Your Real Estate Business?

Scaling isn't just about buying more properties—it's about creating a sustainable and replicable system that generates steady cash flow and builds long-term wealth. Scaling can:

1. Increase Cash Flow: With more properties, monthly rental income increases, strengthening cash flow and financial security.

2.	Diversify Risk: A diversified real estate portfolio reduces the risks associated with market fluctuations or property-specific problems.

3.	Leverage Equity: Scaling allows you to leverage the equity in one property to finance future purchases.

4.	Build Systems for Freedom: Efficient systems and outsourcing allow you to focus on growth, strategy, and opportunities instead of day-to-day management.

5.	Achieve Long-Term Wealth: As your portfolio grows, you build equity and capital appreciation that can lead to generational wealth.

Scaling is an ambitious but achievable goal when approached with strategic planning, discipline, and focus.

1. Develop a Clear Vision & Plan

Before you scale, you need a clear understanding of where you want your business to go. A vision provides direction, while a strategic plan provides the roadmap to get there.

Define Your Objectives:

- How many properties are you looking to own in 1 year, 5 years, or 10 years?

- What type of real estate will you focus on—residential, commercial, multifamily, or mixed-use properties?

- Do you want to focus on property flipping, rental income, development, or wholesaling?

Set SMART Goals:

Ensure your goals are:

- Specific: Clearly define what you want to achieve.

- Measurable: Establish ways to track progress.

- Achievable: Set realistic goals based on your financials and resources.

- Relevant: Ensure your goals align with your long-term vision.

- Time-Bound: Create deadlines for accountability.

Example Goal:

"I want to acquire 10 residential rental properties within the next 5 years by focusing on multifamily apartment buildings in up-and-coming markets."

Strategic Planning for Scaling:

1. Analyze Your Current Portfolio:

- Identify strengths, weaknesses, opportunities, and risks in your current portfolio.

2. Create a Growth Timeline:

- Establish a timeline with milestones for acquiring properties, building partnerships, and implementing new strategies.

3. Build a Business Model:

- Outline your strategy for growth, whether you'll focus on leveraging equity, accessing private financing, joint ventures, or entering new markets.

2. Leverage Financing Strategies

Scaling your real estate business often requires access to financing. As you grow, you'll need strategies to acquire funding to support your purchases, renovations, and operational costs.

Common Financing Options for Scaling:

1. Conventional Bank Financing:

- Traditional mortgages are great if you have a strong credit score and cash reserves.

2. Hard Money Loans:

- These are short-term, higher-interest loans that can provide quick access to capital, especially for flipping properties.

3. Private Lenders & Partnerships:

- Establish relationships with private lenders or partners to access capital without traditional loan restrictions.

4. Home Equity Lines of Credit (HELOCs):

- Use the equity in existing properties as leverage to finance future purchases.

5. Seller Financing:

- Negotiate with sellers to finance part of the property purchase, creating a win-win situation.

6. Commercial Financing:

- As your portfolio grows, commercial financing options become available for multifamily units, mixed-use spaces, or other larger investments.

Pro Tip: Leverage creative financing strategies such as lease options, seller financing, and private equity to overcome market barriers and maximize your cash flow.

3. Build a High-Performance Team

Scaling your real estate business requires more than just financial resources—you'll need a strong support team. Delegating responsibilities to experts allows you to focus on growth while ensuring your business runs smoothly.

Key Members of a Real Estate Scaling Team:

1. Real Estate Agents/Brokers:

- Build relationships with experienced agents to help identify and acquire profitable properties.

2. Property Managers:

- Hire competent property managers to handle day-to-day operations, tenant screening, and maintenance.

3. Accountants & Financial Advisors:

- Ensure taxes are filed efficiently and finances are optimized. An experienced accountant can help minimize tax liability.

4. Legal Advisors:

- Protect your business by working with real estate attorneys for contracts, partnerships, zoning, and dispute resolution.

5. Contractors & Renovation Experts:

- Reliable contractors are essential for ensuring renovation costs and timelines align with your goals.

6. Marketing Specialists:

- A marketing team can help you attract tenants, investors, or off-market properties through branding, advertising, and digital outreach.

Why Delegation is Key to Scaling:

Delegating allows you to focus on strategy, opportunities, and long-term goals rather than getting stuck in daily operational details. A well-structured team streamlines decision-making and fosters scalability.

4. Optimize & Automate Your Systems

Scalability relies on consistency and efficiency. Without streamlined systems and technology, growth can become chaotic and unsustainable.

Implement Property Management Software:

Tools like Buildium, AppFolio, or Rentec Direct allow you to:

- Automate rent collection.

- Track tenant lease expirations and maintenance requests.

- Monitor finances and generate reports.

Adopt Digital Tools for Marketing & Data Analysis:

- Use CRMs (Customer Relationship Management systems) to track leads, investor outreach, and communication.

- Implement market analysis software to identify lucrative areas or trends.

Outsource Routine Tasks:

Delegate administrative tasks (bookkeeping, data entry, marketing campaigns) to virtual assistants or specialized firms. This ensures you can focus on high-level growth strategies.

5. Explore Strategic Partnerships

Strategic partnerships can accelerate growth by leveraging shared resources, expertise, or capital.

Common Partnership Strategies:

1. Joint Ventures: Partner with other investors to split acquisition costs, renovations, and profits.

2. Equity Partnerships: Offer ownership stakes in properties to attract investors in exchange for capital.

3. Cross-Promotion with Real Estate Agents: Build partnerships with real estate agents specializing in different geographic markets.

4. Private Equity Groups: Collaborate with investor groups to access pooled capital for large-scale projects.

6. Enter New Markets & Asset Classes

Scaling isn't just about buying more properties in the same market. Diversify by exploring:

- Different geographic areas with growth potential.

- Diversified property types, such as residential, commercial, multifamily, and industrial real estate.

Geographic diversification can shield your business from regional economic downturns and help you tap into new revenue streams.

Conclusion

Scaling your real estate business is a strategic journey. By developing a vision, leveraging financing options, building a strong team, optimizing systems, and exploring partnerships, you can transform a small real estate operation into a powerful, wealth-building empire.

Real estate scaling requires patience, strategy, discipline, and continuous learning, but the rewards are well worth the effort. As you scale, you'll not only build financial freedom for yourself but also create a legacy that can support future generations.

CHAPTER 10: AVOIDING COMMON PITFALLS

Scaling and building a real estate empire is an exciting journey, but it is not without its challenges. Many investors stumble into common pitfalls that can derail their progress, drain their resources, and hinder their success. Avoiding these mistakes is critical for ensuring the longevity of your real estate investments and maintaining profitability.

This chapter will explore the most common real estate investment and management mistakes, outline how they can impact your business, and provide actionable strategies to help you steer clear of these challenges.

1. Underestimating Costs

One of the most common pitfalls in real estate investing is underestimating costs. New investors, in particular, may fail to account for the many expenses associated with property ownership, renovation, maintenance, financing, and operational costs.

Common Costs Investors Often Overlook:

1. Renovation Costs:

- Unexpected repairs during property renovations can quickly escalate beyond the initial budget. Always budget for contingencies.

2. Maintenance Costs:

- Properties require regular maintenance to maintain their value and attract quality tenants. HVAC systems, plumbing, roof repairs, and other periodic maintenance can add up.

3. Property Management Fees:

- Hiring a property manager comes with costs that can impact your bottom line, but their expertise can save time and stress.

4. Vacancy Costs:

- A vacant property means no rental income. Factor in the costs of covering mortgage payments during the transition between tenants.

5. Taxes & Insurance:

- Property taxes and insurance rates can increase over time, so it's vital to plan accordingly.

6. Financing Costs:

- Interest rates, loan origination fees, and other financing charges can affect cash flow if they are not planned for.

How to Avoid This Pitfall:

- Always budget conservatively by overestimating costs rather than underestimating them.

- Use detailed financial models to account for all potential expenses and unexpected market shifts.

- Build a buffer fund (e.g., 10-20% of your budget) to handle unexpected expenses.

2. Failing to Do Proper Market Research

Investing in the wrong market or failing to analyze trends can lead to poor investment decisions. Many investors rush into opportunities without fully understanding the market landscape.

Red Flags of Poor Market Research:

1. Investing in areas without demand for rental housing or insufficient job opportunities.

2. Overlooking population growth trends, infrastructure development, or local government policies.

3. Relying solely on hearsay rather than verified data.

Strategies to Improve Market Research:

1. Study Demographics: Look for areas with growing populations and job opportunities.

2. Analyze Market Trends: Evaluate rent growth, vacancy rates, and the historical performance of similar property investments.

3. Research Local Infrastructure Projects: Upcoming projects (e.g., highways, public transportation, schools, or corporate investments) can significantly influence property value.

4. Connect with Local Experts: Partner with local real estate agents, market analysts, and property managers who can offer insights.

3. Ignoring Due Diligence

Skipping due diligence is a costly mistake that can lead to purchasing properties with hidden problems. Many investors fail to thoroughly inspect properties or review financials before signing the dotted line.

Key Components of Due Diligence:

1. Property Inspections:

•   Hire a professional inspector to assess the structure, HVAC system, roof, electrical, plumbing, and foundation.

2. Title Search:

•   Ensure there are no liens, encumbrances, or disputes associated with the property's title.

3. Financial Review:

•   Review income statements, mortgage terms, tax history, and operational expenses.

4. Tenant Verification:

•   For properties with existing tenants, ensure the leases are valid and that tenants are financially reliable.

How to Avoid This Pitfall:

Always hire professionals (inspectors, lawyers, and accountants) to perform due diligence. Never rely solely on your intuition.

4. Over-leverage and Poor Financial Management

While leveraging is a powerful tool in real estate investing, overleverage (borrowing too much debt) can put your entire business at risk if markets turn unfavorable or income streams fail.

Signs You May Be Overleveraged:

1. High debt-to-income ratio.

2. Cash flow is tight, leaving no room to handle unexpected expenses.

3. Debt repayment schedules are overly aggressive.

Strategies to Manage Debt Effectively:

1. Maintain Healthy Cash Reserves:

- Keep 6 months to 12 months of mortgage payments in a reserve account to weather market fluctuations or periods of high vacancies.

2. Focus on Positive Cash Flow:

- Ensure rental income consistently exceeds debt obligations.

3.	Diversify Your Portfolio:

•	Avoid putting all your investments into a single asset class or geographic area to reduce risk exposure.

4.	Negotiate Better Financing Terms:

•	Always shop around for financing with favorable terms and manageable repayment schedules.

5. Ignoring Tenant Screening

Tenant turnover, unpaid rent, and property damage are costly problems for landlords. Poor tenant screening leads to financial losses and headaches.

Key Elements of a Successful Screening Process:

1.	Criminal Background Checks: Prevent conflicts with high-risk tenants.

2.	Employment & Income Verification: Tenants should make enough income to comfortably pay rent.

3.	Rental References: Reach out to previous landlords to verify payment habits and care for property.

4.	Credit History Review: Evaluate financial responsibility through credit checks.

How to Avoid This Pitfall:

Implement strict, fair, and legal tenant screening procedures. Use consistent criteria for every applicant to comply with fair housing laws.

6. Neglecting Property Maintenance

Ignoring maintenance is a shortcut to larger, costlier problems. Deferred maintenance can lead to issues that make properties less marketable and lower their value.

Common Maintenance Pitfalls:

1. Allowing small problems (e.g., a leaky roof) to become emergencies.

2. Failing to inspect appliances, HVAC systems, or other critical features regularly.

3. Delaying routine inspections.

How to Avoid This Pitfall:

1. Establish a regular preventive maintenance schedule.

2. Hire professional contractors for inspections and maintenance to ensure everything runs smoothly.

3. Respond promptly to tenant maintenance requests to preserve tenant satisfaction.

7. Failing to Adapt to Market Changes

The real estate market is dynamic. Economic downturns, shifts in demographics, changes in zoning laws, and evolving technology can affect your investment strategy.

How to Stay Agile in Changing Markets:

1.   Monitor economic trends (unemployment rates, interest rates, consumer demand).

2.   Invest in diversification across asset classes and markets.

3.   Embrace innovation by implementing tech solutions or exploring emerging trends like smart homes or shared housing models.

Conclusion

The journey to building your property empire involves strategic planning, learning, and adaptability. Avoiding common pitfalls like underestimating costs, skipping due diligence, failing to research, over-leveraging, neglecting maintenance, or ignoring market trends can save you time, money, and frustration

Real estate success is about learning from mistakes, building resilient strategies, and ensuring you plan for both opportunities and challenges. By implementing the strategies outlined in this chapter, you'll strengthen your foundation, make more informed decisions, and ensure your journey to building wealth through real estate is both profitable and sustainable.

Congratulations! You've made it to the end of Unlocking Real Estate: A Practical Guide to Building Your Property Empire. This journey has equipped you with the knowledge, strategies, and tools needed to build, scale, and manage your real estate investments effectively.

Real estate is much more than just buying and selling properties—it's about strategy, perseverance, and financial intelligence. From understanding the market and financing your first property to negotiating like a pro and scaling your business, this book has provided a comprehensive roadmap to navigate the complexities of real estate investing.

Key Takeaways from Your Journey

1. Understanding the Fundamentals: Real estate begins with knowing the market, financial terms, and investment opportunities. Your foundation is your greatest strength, and this knowledge sets the stage for success.

2. Choosing the Right Strategy: Whether through buy-and-hold, flipping, development, or multifamily investing, selecting the strategy that aligns with your goals is crucial for long-term profitability.

3. Financing Is a Pathway to Growth: Leveraging the right financing options can be the key to expanding your portfolio without exhausting your resources.

4.   The Art of Negotiation: Mastering negotiation ensures you secure the best deals, maximize profit, and protect your investments.

5.   Systems Matter: Scaling your real estate business requires the implementation of efficient systems, technology, and partnerships. Delegation allows you to focus on strategy, growth, and opportunities.

6.   Avoiding Pitfalls: Knowledge of common real estate mistakes—ranging from poor market research to underestimating costs—ensures that you stay ahead of risks and setbacks.

7.   Managing Properties for Success: Managing properties effectively involves maintaining tenant relationships, preserving property value, and optimizing cash flow.

The Next Step on Your Journey

Building a property empire isn't a destination—it's a journey that requires continuous learning, adaptation, and action. As you put the strategies from this book into practice, remember:

•   Take action: Knowledge without action will only take you so far. Start small, learn as you grow, and take calculated risks.

- Learn from every experience: Every property, every negotiation, and every challenge will teach you something new. Embrace these lessons as opportunities to improve.

- Stay agile: The market is always evolving. Success requires flexibility, innovation, and the ability to pivot when opportunities arise.

Final Thoughts

Building wealth through real estate is about more than just money. It's about creating financial freedom, building a legacy, and having the ability to live life on your own terms. The tools are now in your hands—the question is, what will you do with them?

Remember, real estate is a journey of patience, discipline, and vision. Whether you're just starting out or building upon an existing portfolio, the road to success starts with belief in yourself and your goals.

Now, go out there and unlock the full potential of your real estate journey. Your property empire awaits.

Here's to your success in real estate. 🏡💼

ABOUT THE AUTHOR

Armando Marichalar is a rising star in the world of literature, poised to make a significant impact with his unique voice, compelling storytelling, and insightful perspectives. Born and raised in a small town nestled in the heart of the countryside, Armando's passion for writing was ignited at a young age as he found solace and inspiration in the pages of books.

Armando's journey as an author began as a personal quest for self-expression and creativity—a journey fueled by a deep-seated desire to share stories that resonate with readers on a profound level. Drawing inspiration from his own life experiences, as well as the rich tapestry of human emotions and relationships, Armando weaves narratives that are both timeless and universal, capturing the complexities of the human experience with honesty, depth, and authenticity.

With a background in psychology and a keen interest in exploring the intricacies of the human psyche, Armando brings a unique perspective to his writing, delving into the depths of human emotion, motivation, and behavior with empathy, insight, and sensitivity. His characters are vividly drawn, multi-dimensional beings who grapple with love, loss, hope, and redemption, navigating the complexities of life with courage, resilience, and grace.

Armando's writing style is characterized by its lyrical prose, evocative imagery, and thought-provoking themes that resonate long after the final page has been turned. His stories are imbued with a sense of wonder, curiosity, and wonderment, inviting readers on a journey of self-discovery, introspection, and transformation.

As a new author in the making, Armando is excited to embark on this literary journey, eager to connect with readers from all walks of life and to inspire, entertain, and uplift through the power of storytelling. With a steadfast commitment to excellence, a passion for creativity, and a boundless imagination, Armando is poised to make a lasting impact on the literary landscape and to leave an indelible mark on the hearts and minds of readers everywhere.

In his free time, Armando enjoys immersing himself in nature, exploring new cultures, and seeking inspiration in the world around him. He believes in the transformative power of art, literature, and storytelling to inspire change, foster empathy, and unite humanity in our shared journey through life.

Armando Marichalar is a name to watch in the world of literature—a fresh voice, a bold talent, and a storyteller for the ages. As he embarks on this exciting new chapter in his journey as an author, the world eagerly awaits the stories that he will share and the impact that he will make on the literary landscape.

www.ingramcontent.com/pod-product-compliance
Lightning Source LLC
Chambersburg PA
CBHW071039240526
45469CB00006BD/2273